Library of Congress Catalog Card Number: 60-9385

Printed in the United States of America

B C D E

LET'S FIND OUT

WHAT
ELECTRICITY
DOES

by

MARTHA and CHARLES SHAPP

illustrated by Ida Scheib

FRANKLIN WATTS, INC.
575 LEXINGTON AVENUE
NEW YORK

Once there was a boy named
Aladdin.

Aladdin had a magic lamp.

When Aladdin wanted something,
he rubbed the lamp.

Out came a genie!

Aladdin told the genie what he
wanted.

ABRACADABRA!

The genie did whatever Aladdin
wanted.

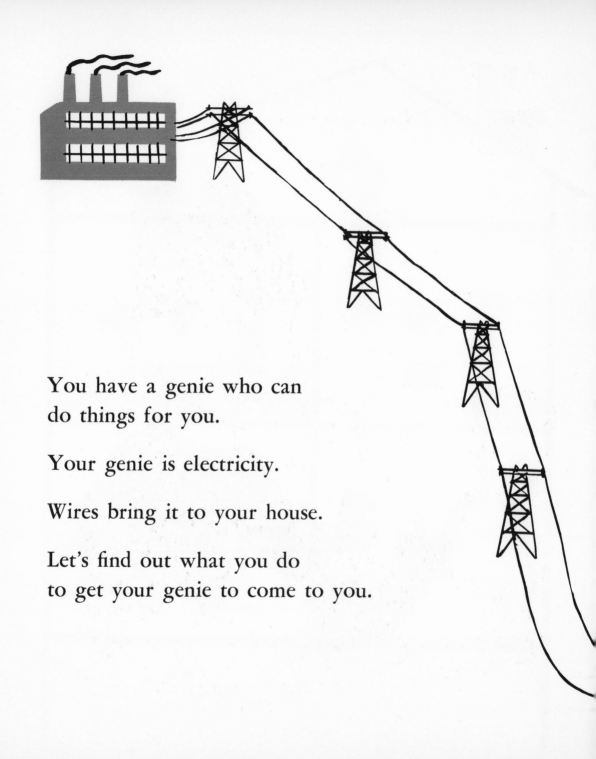

You have a genie who can
do things for you.

Your genie is electricity.

Wires bring it to your house.

Let's find out what you do
to get your genie to come to you.

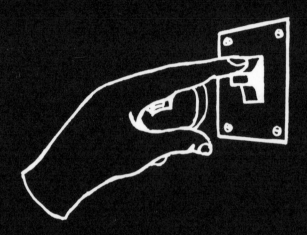

Your genie comes when you flick a
switch.

Your genie comes when you turn a
dial.

When it is dark, you flick a switch
and . . .

ABRACADABRA . . . the genie brings you
light.

When you want a TV program,
you turn a dial and . . .

ABRACADABRA ... there's your
program.

Electricity cooks your food.

Electricity keeps your food cool and fresh.

Electricity can make your house warm.

It can make your house cool.

You can talk to somebody far, far
away.

Electricity makes the telephone work.

Electricity tells you when to get up.

It tells you when somebody is at the
door.

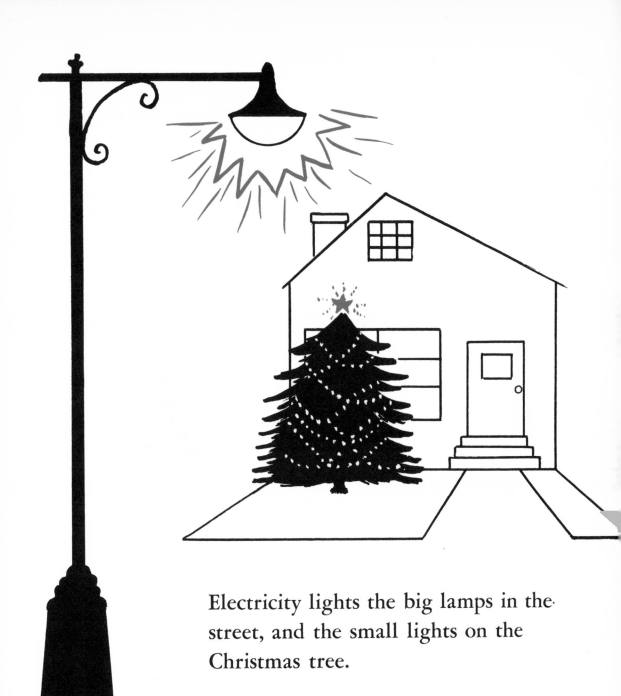

Electricity lights the big lamps in the street, and the small lights on the Christmas tree.

Electricity makes things easier to do.

Which is easier,

this . . .

or this?

Which is easier,

this . . .

or this?

Isn't this easier than . . .

this?

Electricity helps in other ways.

It can help cut your hair.

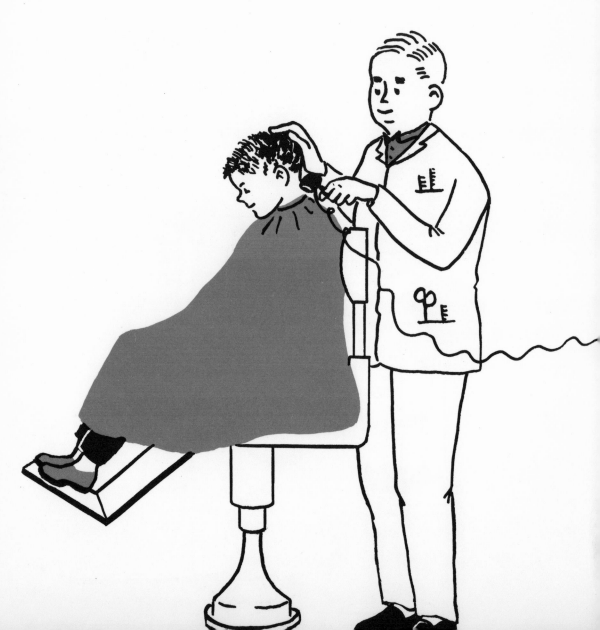

It helps fix your teeth.

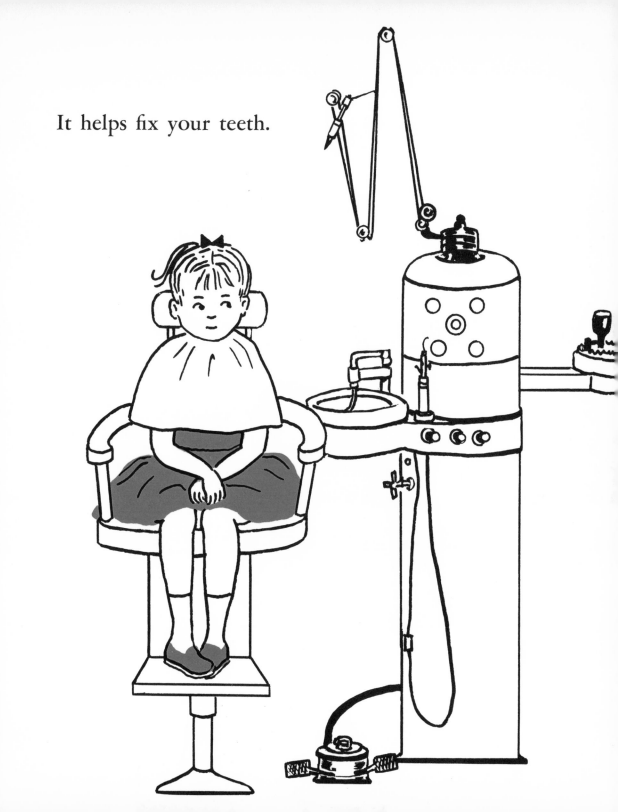

Electricity can help father shave.

It can help dry mother's hair.

Electricity can move things.

It moves small trains.

It moves big trains.

Electricity can move you
round and round.

It can move you up and down.

Flick a switch, turn a dial.

That's all you have to do

To make electricity

Go to work for you.

VOCABULARY LIST (100 words)

Of these, 43 appear in the other *Let's Find Out* books: *What's Big and What's Small,*
What the Signs Say, What's Light and What's Heavy.

a	far	make(s)
abracadabra	father	mother's
Aladdin	find	move(s)
all	fix	
and	flick	named
at	food	
away	for	on
	fresh	once
		or
big		other
boy	genie	out
brings	get	
	go	
		program
came	had	
can	hair	round
Christmas	have	rubbed
come(s)	he	
cooks	help(s)	shave
cool	house	small
cut		somebody
	in	something
dark	is	street
dial	isn't	switch
did	it	
do		talk
door	keeps	teeth
down		telephone
dry	lamp(s)	tells
	let's	than
	light(s)	that's
easier		the
electricity	magic	

there('s)	up	which
things		who
this	want(ed)	wires
to	warm	work
told	was	
trains	ways	you
tree	what	your
turn	whatever	
TV	when